C000311126

Contents

Front cover **BODMIN PARKWAY:** The only surviving London & South Western Railway 'T9' 4-4-0 locomotive, No 30120, makes a very impressive sight at Bodmin Parkway station on 22 October 2010. The 'T9' is one of two ex-LSWR locomotives owned by the National Railway Museum and on long-term loan to the Bodmin & Wenford Railway. *Martin Creese*

Title page **QUARRY CURVE:** A pair of Great Western Railway 'small Prairie' tank engines, Nos 5526 and 5521, approach the summit of the Bodmin & Wenford Railway at 'Quarry Curve' on 17 April 2010 at the head of a train from Bodmin Parkway to Bodmin General. *Brian Aston*

Acknowledgments

Several people contributed material freely for consideration for publication in this book, to whom the author is extremely grateful. The quality of the images submitted was such that choosing those to include – not least to ensure a good variety of locomotives, trains and locations – was no easy task. There was enough for a second book! Considerable effort has gone into researching the information for the captions that accompany the photographs, but if any mistakes have 'slipped the net' the responsibility for these is mine, and mine alone! Above all, I am full of admiration for all those who, over the last 25-plus years, have given freely of their time and money to establish the Bodmin & Wenford Railway and help to make it the real success story that it is today – it is a pleasure to lead such a great team of people. This book is by way of a tribute to all of them.

Richard Jones

About the author

Richard Jones has been actively involved with heritage railways, largely, in the West Country for over 40 years. Starting as a volunteer on the (then) Dart Valley Railway in 1973, he has been actively involved with the West Somerset Railway since 1977 in a variety of roles. After an 18-year career in the teaching profession, Richard became a full-time railwayman and, since 2000, has worked in both the main line and heritage railway sectors. He was General Manager of the Bodmin & Wenford Railway from 2008-13, a period where the line enjoyed significant growth and success, before moving on to a similar role at the Swanage Railway, and is currently the Keighley & Worth Valley Railway's Operations Manager.

All rights reserved. No part of this publication may be reproduced, stored in a retrieval system or transmitted, in any form or by any means, electronic, mechanical, photocopying, recording or otherwise, without prior permission in writing from Silver Link Publishing Ltd.

British Library Cataloguing in Publication Data
A catalogue record for this book is available from the British Library.

Printed and bound in Ceská Republika

© Richard Jones, 2012

First published in 2012
Reprinted 2016

ISBN 978 1 85794 390 0

Silver Link Publishing Ltd
The Trundle
Ringstead Road
Great Addington
Kettering
Northants NN14 4BW

Tel/Fax: 01536 330588
email: sales@nostalgiacollection.com
Website: www.nostalgiacollection.com

Introduction

The Bodmin & Wenford Railway (BWR) grew from the early commitment and enthusiasm of a small group of individuals who were determined to reopen a Cornish branch line and operate it as a tourist and leisure attraction, predominantly using steam locomotives. It is an absolute gem!

The railway, which now attracts around 60,000 passengers each year, proudly boasts that it offers its visitors the opportunity – unique in the Duchy – to discover the excitement and nostalgia of steam travel with a journey back in time on Cornwall's only standard gauge railway still regularly operated by steam locomotives.

In the busy and increasingly electronic and satellite world in which we all now live, the BWR offers its passengers the chance to relax in style and enjoy a leisurely 13-mile return trip through beautiful countryside, taking in the sights, sounds and smells of a bygone age, as the era of a Cornish branch line in the 1950s reveals itself during the course of their journey.

The Bodmin branch line was authorised by Act of Parliament on 10 August 1882. The first sod was cut in March 1884 and the line opened from Bodmin Road (now Bodmin Parkway) to Bodmin, a distance of 3½ miles, on 27 May 1887, built to standard gauge (4ft 8½in).

A further line, from Bodmin to Boscarne Junction, a distance of 3 miles, was opened in September 1888 to connect with the existing Bodmin & Wadebridge Railway, which had opened back in 1834 (running from Wadebridge to Wenfordbridge, with a branch to Bodmin). The Bodmin & Wadebridge line was one of the first railways in the world to use steam locomotives, and certainly the first in Cornwall, and was taken over by the London & South Western Railway in 1847.

The 6½ miles of track that now forms the BWR was closed by British Railways to passengers in January 1967, and completely in 1983. Efforts to preserve the branch line, with a view to reopening it as a heritage steam railway, began shortly after closure, and the Bodmin Railway Preservation Society (BRPS) was formed in July 1984. In a bid to raise the £139,600 needed to purchase the line from Bodmin Parkway to Boscarne Junction, via Bodmin General, the Bodmin & Wenford Railway plc was formed by the society. The company successfully purchased the track, and North Cornwall District Council (now part of Cornwall Council) secured the land, from British Rail. The first Open Day was held on Sunday 1 June 1986, when a small steam locomotive – former Devonport Dockyard 0-4-0ST No 19 – performed shunting demonstrations at Bodmin General station. These were the first official train movements in the preservation era, and thus the Bodmin & Wenford Railway is proud to celebrate its 25th anniversary in 2011.

Since then the railway has gone from strength to strength. The photographs contained within the pages of this book not only illustrate the unique and quintessential charm of this Cornish branch line, but also the picturesque scenery through which the line travels and the wide variety of locomotives that have traversed its tracks over the past quarter of a century.

So, relax and enjoy this journey in photographs along the Bodmin & Wenford Railway...

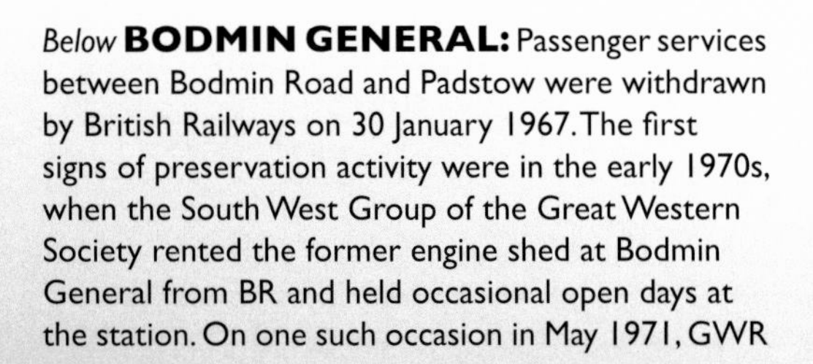

Below **BODMIN GENERAL:** Passenger services between Bodmin Road and Padstow were withdrawn by British Railways on 30 January 1967. The first signs of preservation activity were in the early 1970s, when the South West Group of the Great Western Society rented the former engine shed at Bodmin General from BR and held occasional open days at the station. On one such occasion in May 1971, GWR '1361' Class 0-6-0ST No 1363 – which spent all its working life at nearby Plymouth (Laira) shed – is seen with Hawksworth brake coach No 7372. Note the single-road engine shed in the background, which was later demolished by BR. The GWS later vacated the site and moved its stock to a new base at Didcot in Oxfordshire. *Bernard Mills*

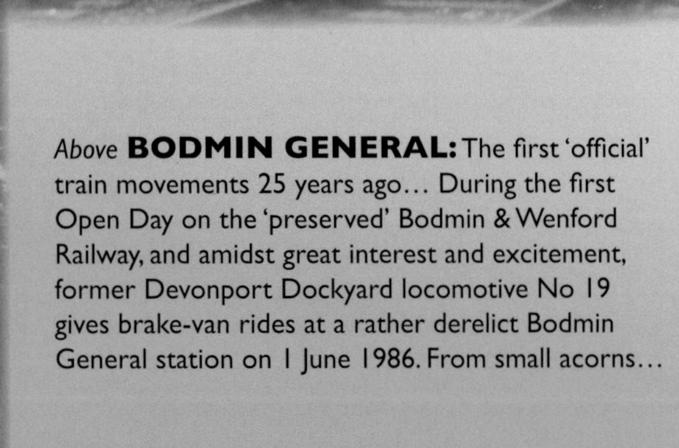

Above **BODMIN GENERAL:** The first 'official' train movements 25 years ago... During the first Open Day on the 'preserved' Bodmin & Wenford Railway, and amidst great interest and excitement, former Devonport Dockyard locomotive No 19 gives brake-van rides at a rather derelict Bodmin General station on 1 June 1986. From small acorns...

Right **CHARLIE'S GATE:** No 19 was a consistent and reliable performer in the early years of the Bodmin & Wenford Railway, and for most of 1990 was the only steam locomotive available for service! Built by W. G. Bagnall Ltd at its Castle Engine Works at Stafford in 1950, it was the last steam locomotive built for use in Devonport Dockyard, where it spent 19 years shunting around the docks area. After purchase for preservation, No 19 left the Dockyard in 1969 and was based at Bugle for several years. Owned by the Cornish Steam Locomotive Preservation Society (CSLPS), it was the first locomotive to work on the BWR (see the photograph opposite), before moving permanently to Bodmin in 1987. On a lovely late spring afternoon, the small saddle tank is seen climbing the gradient past Charlie's Gate with the 5pm service from Bodmin Parkway on 31 May 1991. *Bernard Mills*

Left **BODMIN PARKWAY:** Bodmin Parkway (formerly Bodmin Road) is the southern terminus of the Bodmin & Wenford Railway, with trains running into the former branch-line platform on the up side of the station. 'USA'-type 0-6-0T No 30075 made a three-week visit to the railway in September 1993. Very similar in design to the former Southern Railway class, No 30075 was actually built by Yugoslavian Railways in 1960, and purchased for preservation in Britain in 1990. The locomotive awaits departure from Bodmin Parkway on 4 September 1993. *Brian Aston*

Below far left **BODMIN PARKWAY:** A friendly face greets visitors at Bodmin Parkway! Hunslet 0-6-0T *The Lady Armaghdale*, built in 1898, masquerades as the famous Blue Engine during a 'Day Out With Thomas' event on 14 August 2002. The locomotive is currently on static display in The Engine House at Highley on the Severn Valley Railway, where it has been based since being purchased for preservation in 1969 – a far cry from its 65-year working life on the Manchester Ship Canal railway network! *Brian Aston*

Left **BODMIN PARKWAY:** The railway's beautifully turned-out BR(W) auto-trailer No W232W – which returned to service in April 2011 after an extensive two-year restoration carried out at the railway's own workshop at Bodmin General – awaits departure from 'Parkway' (as the station is often referred to) on a private charter working on 10 July 2011. GWR '64xx' 0-6-0PT No 6435 is at the head of the train. Both the locomotive and carriage are owned by the Bodmin & Wenford Railway Trust, the 'charitable arm' of the railway. Note the promotional sign to the right of the photograph – see the back cover. *Richard Jones*

Below **BODMIN PARKWAY:** The diminutive Ruston diesel shunter No 3 *Lec* – one of the least photographed engines on the line! – performs shunting duties at Bodmin Parkway on 21 November 2007. The locomotive was built in 1960 and used by Lec Refrigeration at its Bognor Regis plant, and has been based at Bodmin since October 1988. No 3 is now named *Brian* in memory of the late Brian Shadwick, its former owner who did so much to return the shunter to working order. The carriage is an absolute gem – a clerestory 'Royal' coach built by the Great Western Railway at Swindon in 1881, and the oldest surviving standard gauge bogie carriage still on its original underframe in the country. It was built as a special saloon for private hire, and used by various celebrities of the time, including the Prince of Wales, later to become King Edward VII. It is now undergoing restoration. *Brian Aston*

Above **BODMIN PARKWAY:** The only surviving pair of Beattie well tank locomotives, Nos 30585 and 30587, make a superb sight on demonstration goods trains at Bodmin Parkway on 5 October 2007. The original class of 85 engines were built for the London & South Western Railway between 1863 and 1875, originally to work London suburban trains. Most of the class were withdrawn by 1899, but three 'Beatties' were retained and based locally at Wadebridge shed for more than 60 years, where they were used regularly on station pilot duties and on the tightly curved branch line to Wenfordbridge. No 30587 is owned by the National Railway Museum and is on long-term loan to the Bodmin & Wenford Railway. *Brian Aston*

Below **BODMIN PARKWAY:** Southern Railway 'West Country' 4-6-2 No 34007 *Wadebridge* was based on the line for a number of years during its restoration from scrapyard condition. Designed by O.V. S. Bulleid and built at Brighton Works in 1945, the locomotive makes a splendid sight at the head of its 'Return to Steam Special' on 29 October 2006. The original Bulleid 'Pacifics' were once a regular sight during the 1950s and early '60s on the former North Cornwall line, which closed in October 1966. No 34007 is now based on the Mid-Hants Railway. *Bernard Mills*

Above **BODMIN PARKWAY:** A brace of GWR tank engines, 0-6-0ST No 813 and 0-6-0PT No 4612, both proudly bearing 'GREAT WESTERN' on the side of their tanks – start the 3½-mile climb to Bodmin General on 7 September 2002, during the railway's annual late-summer Steam Gala event. No 813 has a very interesting history, having been built by Hudswell Clarke & Company of Leeds in 1900 and once owned by the Port Talbot Railway Company in South Wales. In 1934 the locomotive was bought for colliery use by Backworth Collieries Ltd of Northumberland and, after more than 40 years there, was saved for preservation in 1967 and moved to the Severn Valley Railway, where it has been based ever since. No 4612 is a regular and popular member of the BWR steam fleet. *Brian Aston*

BODMIN PARKWAY: The broad gauge (7ft 0¼in) Cornwall Railway was opened between Plymouth and Truro in 1859. It had a station at Bodmin Road (as it was originally called) and became part of the Great Western Railway in 1876. Eleven years later it became a junction station, following the opening of the Bodmin branch on 27 May 1887. Since 1990 the Bodmin & Wenford Railway has run regular passenger services to Bodmin Parkway, using the same branch-line platform. Connections can be made with services on the national network and, while the majority of trains on the main line are now diesel-hauled, steam-hauled charter trains still make an occasional appearance!

Below left **BODMIN ROAD:** Class 25 No 25080 eases its seven-coach train off the branch and over the junction to the up main line at Bodmin Road with a special charter train returning to Derby on 30 September 1978. This was a 'final farewell train' following closure of the line to Wadebridge earlier that month. *Bernard Mills*

Above **BODMIN PARKWAY:** GWR 'Castle' Class 4-6-0 No 5029 *Nunney Castle* makes a spirited departure southbound from Bodmin Parkway with a main-line charter train on 10 July 2011, appropriately carrying 'The Cornishman' headboard. The Bodmin branch can be glimpsed in the left distance, while the line in the left foreground is the 'Exchange Siding', which offers a physical connection between the BWR and the main-line network. *Richard Jones*

Left **BODMIN ROAD:** A busy scene at Bodmin Road station on 11 May 1968. Note the various station buildings, most now long-since demolished, though the footbridge and signal box remain, the latter now serving as the Station Cafe and operated by the Bodmin & Wenford Railway. *Bernard Mills*

GWR TANK ENGINES: The majority of passenger services on the Bodmin & Wenford Railway are worked by an impressive quartet of former Great Western Railway tank engines, as illustrated here.

Below **CHARLIE'S GATE:** No 6435 is the only one of the quartet of GWR locomotives based at Bodmin that did not end up in a scrapyard after withdrawal, being purchased for preservation directly from British Railways in 1965. The '64xx' Class pannier tanks were found on most parts of the Great Western system and were fitted for working push-pull (auto) trains. They were a regular sight on such duties from Plymouth into east Cornwall for many years. No 6435 spent many years working on the Dart Valley Railway, before being purchased by the Bodmin & Wenford Railway Trust in 2008. The locomotive makes a splendid sight, together with the newly restored auto-coach No W232W, passing Charlie's Gate on 10 April 2011. *Bernard Mills*

Above **QUARRY CURVE:** GWR '57xx' Class 0-6-0PT No 4612 was one of a class of 863 such locomotives built between 1929 and 1950. They were used for shunting and light mixed-traffic duties over virtually the entire Great Western system, including Cornwall, earning themselves a reputation as strong and free-steaming. No 4612 was built at Swindon Works in 1942 and spent the majority of its career with the GWR and BR working in the Bristol and Swindon areas. Initially purchased for preservation in 1981, the pannier tank was bought by the Bodmin & Wenford Railway Trust and returned to steam in July 2001. It has been a regular on BWR services ever since. No 4612 rounds Quarry Curve with a train from Bodmin Parkway on 14 March 2009. *Audrey Mills*

Below **BODMIN GENERAL:** GWR '42xx' 2-8-0T No 4247 is the largest and heaviest steam locomotive based on the line. This powerful class was designed primarily to work heavy short-haul coal trains in South Wales. However, No 4247 is another BWR-based locomotive with a 'Cornish pedigree' as, between November 1952 and January 1958, it was based at St Blazey shed to work china clay trains, primarily to the docks at Fowey and Par. After withdrawal by British Railways in August 1964, and after spending more than 20 years in the scrapyard at Barry, the 2-8-0T was purchased for preservation in 1985. Owned by 4247 Limited, and on a long-term agreement with the BWR Trust, No 4247 has been based at Bodmin since 2005. The size of the locomotive can be appreciated in this view at Bodmin General on 14 August 2008. *Richard Jones*

Above **CHARLIE'S GATE:** GWR '4575' Class 2-6-2T No 5552 heads past Charlie's Gate on 5 June 2004 with a special charter train. The locomotive was built at Swindon in 1928 at a cost of £3,578. These 'small Prairie' tanks were a regular sight on branch lines in Devon and Cornwall, and worked the majority of services between Bodmin Road and Wadebridge for more than 40 years. No 5552's last five years prior to withdrawal by British Railways in October 1960 were spent based at Truro shed. After covering nearly 900,000 miles in service, the locomotive spent 25 years in a South Wales scrapyard before being purchased for preservation at Bodmin in 1986. After an extensive restoration, No 5552 returned to service in September 2003. *Brian Aston*

LSWR LOCOMOTIVES: The Bodmin & Wenford Railway is honoured to have been entrusted with the future care of two locomotives owned by the National Railway Museum at York. Both were built originally for the London & South Western Railway (LSWR) and are truly iconic locomotives of the Victorian age, and both have a genuine Cornish pedigree!

CHARLIE'S GATE: LSWR 'T9' Class 4-4-0 No 30120 looks a fine sight as it passes Charlie's Gate with a Bodmin Parkway to Bodmin General train composed of carmine-and-cream-liveried coaches on 10 October 2010. The 'T9' Class once totalled 66 engines, designed for the LSWR by Dugald Drummond and introduced in 1899 – No 30120 is the only survivor. The locomotives became known as 'Greyhounds' due to their good turn of speed. Towards the end of steam they were a regular sight on the former 'Withered Arm' lines in the West Country, working from Okehampton to Bude, Wadebridge and Padstow. After an extensive overhaul funded by the BWR Trust, No 30120 triumphantly returned to steam at Bodmin in September 2010. *Graham Hutton*

BOSCARNE BRANCH: Among the oldest standard gauge locomotives inherited by British Railways upon nationalisation in 1948 were three ex-LSWR Beattie well tanks, built in 1874/75, which spent more than 60 years based at Wadebridge on both station pilot duties and working china clay trains on the steeply graded and lightly laid branch to Wenfordbridge, where they proved to be ideally suited. One of the two surviving locomotives, No 30587, returned 'home' to Cornwall in 2002 after an overhaul funded by the BWR Trust, and is a popular member of the railway's steam fleet. Recreating its Wadebridge days, the 'Beattie' works a photographers' charter train on the Boscarne branch on 16 October 2009. *Audrey Mills*

INDUSTRIAL LOCOMOTIVES: In addition to the former British Railways engines, a small number of former industrial locomotives are also based at Bodmin, several having worked in the local area for many years.

Below **BODMIN GENERAL:** A fine portrait of Bagnall 0-4-0ST No 19 stabled on 'Barracks Siding' at Bodmin General on 8 September 2002. No 19 was the last steam locomotive built for use in Devonport Dockyard. In 1986 it became the first steam locomotive to work trains on the 'preserved' Bodmin & Wenford Railway. While now too small to work trains regularly on the line, it is steamed at special events and has made a number of visits to other heritage railways over recent years, 'flying the flag' for the BWR. *Brian Aston*

Right and below right **WEST HEATH:** Perhaps the most famous two locomotives on the line are the 'Port of Par twins', *Alfred* and *Judy*, which were made famous by Rev W. Awdry as the inspiration for his characters Bill and Ben in the original 'Thomas the Tank Engine' books! Both were built by W. G. Bagnall Ltd at Stafford, *Judy* in 1937 and *Alfred* in 1953, and spent all their working lives shunting around Par Docks. They were built with 'cut-down' cabs in order to fit safely under a bridge that carried the Plymouth-Penzance main line over the single track running from the docks to St Blazey yard. Both were reunited in steam at Bodmin in April 2009 for the first time in 40 years at a ceremony attended by Rev Awdry's son, Christopher, who is seen *(left)* on the footplate of *Judy* in the company of BWR staff Martyn Blackwell and Geoff Westlake.

Alfred and *Judy (below)* haul a special train formed of brake-vans at West Heath, on the climb from Boscarne Junction to Bodmin General, on 3 April 2009. *Richard Jones*

Above **BODMIN GENERAL:** A Royal Train on the Bodmin & Wenford! In June 2000 HM The Queen and HRH The Duke of Edinburgh travelled by train from Bodmin Parkway to Bodmin General as part of a series of engagements in the county. The special train was hauled by the immaculately turned-out pairing of 0-6-0ST No 62 *Ugly* and 0-6-0PT No 9682, built by Robert Stephenson & Hawthorn in 1950 and British Railways at Swindon in 1949 respectively. The train was formed of GWR Inspection Saloon No DW80975 and is here seen at Bodmin General after arrival on 8 June 2000. *Brian Aston*

Above right **BODMIN GENERAL:** During the visit, HM The Queen is introduced to Keith Searle, the BWR's first General Manager. *Keith Searle collection*

Right **BODMIN GENERAL:** The Bodmin & Wenford Railway was delighted to welcome a second Royal visitor, HRH The Princess Alexandra KG GCVO, on 4 May 2011. The Princess – who enjoyed a trip on the line's newly restored GWR auto-train during her visit – is seen at Bodmin General in the company of Lady Mary Holborow, the Lord Lieutenant of Cornwall, and the author. *Ben Harding/BWR*

CHARLIE'S GATE: The most popular and well-known photographic location on the Bodmin & Wenford Railway is Charlie's Gate, which lies just off the A38 road about half a mile from Bodmin Parkway. It is believed that the location is so named after the many times the Royal Train was stabled there while carrying members of the Royal Family, including HRH Prince Charles, Duke of Cornwall, to engagements in the Duchy. 'Charlie's Gate' itself offered a convenient location for transfer between train and car when required. With the generous permission of the landowner, the location offers many excellent photographic opportunities.

Left **CHARLIE'S GATE:** Ivatt 2-6-2T No 41312 – masquerading as long-since-scrapped sister engine No 41316 – performs for the cameras on a special charter train for photographers on 3 September 2001, during a short visit to the line that autumn. The locomotive was built by British Railways at Crewe Works in 1952, and between December 1959 and March 1963 worked in the West Country based at Barnstaple Junction shed. It was rescued from Barry scrapyard for preservation in 1974 and is now based on the Mid-Hants Railway. *Brian Aston*

Below **CHARLIE'S GATE:** Dwarfed by the surrounding countryside, LSWR 'T9' 4-4-0 No 30120 climbs away from the Glynn Valley with a typical North Cornwall line mixed train on 21 October 2010. No 30120 was the last of the class to be withdrawn by British Railways in 1963. *Ralph Ward*

Above **CHARLIE'S GATE:** Built by the Great Western Railway in 1903 at a cost of £1,957, No 3717 *City of Truro* is the only surviving member of the 27 'City' Class locomotives built for express passenger work. It achieved notoriety by reputedly being the first locomotive to achieve a recorded speed of 100mph on 9 May 1904. In later years the class became confined to secondary lines. Owned by the National Railway Museum, the locomotive is now based on the Gloucestershire Warwickshire Railway, although it makes frequent visits to other heritage railways. Indeed, No 3717 (previously numbered 3440) has made three visits to the Bodmin & Wenford Railway – in 1992, 2004 and 2011. During its first visit to the line, the iconic engine is seen heading past Charlie's Gate on 30 May 1992. *Bernard Mills*

Top right **CHARLIE'S GATE:** A delightful spring scene sees visiting GWR '14xx' Class 0-4-2T No 1450 and auto-trailer W228W heading up the gradient towards Bodmin General in April 1997. *Audrey Mills*

Above right **CHARLIE'S GATE:** 1950 or 2010...? Perfectly recreating the china clay trains that were once a regular sight on the Bodmin branch, GWR '4575' Class 2-6-2T No 5526 – which was a St Blazey engine in 1928-29, and outstationed at the sub-shed of Bodmin for part of that time – heads a rake of clay wagons, complete with a GWR 'Toad' brake-van at the rear, past Charlie's Gate on a special charter working on 19 April 2010. The BR black-liveried locomotive is based at the South Devon Railway, and was one of a trio of 'small Prairie' tanks in action at the line's Spring Steam Spectacular gala event that year to celebrate the 175th anniversary of the formation of the GWR. *Richard Jones*

B&W 125: The 3½-mile steeply graded and sharply curved branch from Bodmin Road to Bodmin was built by the Great Western Railway and opened on 27 May 1887, and thus celebrates its 125th anniversary in 2012.

Right **BODMIN PARKWAY:** GWR '1366' Class 0-6-0PT No 1369, built at Swindon in 1934 and now the only surviving member of the class, has made several visits to the line from its home at the South Devon Railway. It too is a 'local' engine, having been based at Wadebridge shed from 1962 to 1964, where three members of the class displaced the Beattie well tanks, and was a regular sight on the Wenfordbridge branch during this time. No 1369 is seen climbing away from Bodmin Parkway with a short mixed train on 21 October 2008. To the rear of the train can be seen the parapets of 'Bridge 1', a viaduct carrying the Bodmin branch over the River Fowey. *Sam Felce*

Left **Nr DREASON:** The impressive combination of LSWR Beattie well tank No 30587 and GWR 'small Prairie' tank No 5552 round the curve on the approach to Dreason with an evening service to Bodmin General on 3 September 2010, during the railway's popular annual Steam Gala & Real Ale Festival event. *Graham Hutton*

Right **DREASON:** During its first weekend back in service after an extensive (and expensive!) overhaul, LSWR 'T9' Class 4-4-0 No 30120 – the only surviving member of the class and owned by the National Railway Museum – climbs away from Bodmin Parkway on 3 September 2010. *Brian Aston*

Right **COLESLOGGETT HALT:** In glorious spring light, GWR '42xx' Class 2-8-0T No 4247 heads past Colesloggett Halt as it climbs to Bodmin General with its train of carmine-and-cream carriages on 17 April 2010. The hills in the background rise towards Bodmin Moor. Colesloggett Halt was built and opened by the BWR in 1992 to serve a nearby Farm Park, which sadly later closed. However, a footpath from the Halt leads to Cardinham Woods, a popular local beauty spot. *Sam Felce*

Above **'BRIDGE 3':** The BWR's Great Western auto-train, formed of locomotive No 6435 and trailer W232W, bursts under Bridge 3 – a little-used accommodation bridge – with a photographers' charter train on 10 May 2011. Note the immaculate condition of the permanent way, the track over this part of the line having been re-laid earlier that year following flood damage the previous November. Both the locomotive and auto-coach are in later British Railways livery, typical of the late 1950s/early 1960s. *Peter Zabek*

Right **COLESLOGGETT HALT:** LNER 'V2' Class 2-6-2 No 60800 *Green Arrow* – another locomotive owned by the National Railway Museum, York – spent a short period in May 1999 working on the line in between main-line rail tour duties in Cornwall. With a five-coach train of matching maroon coaches in tow, the BR lined-green locomotive climbs away from Colesloggett Halt on 2 May 1999. No 60800 is believed to be the only LNER engine to have worked on the Bodmin branch to date! *Brian Aston*

Below **'BRIDGE 7':** One of the highlights of the line's Steam Gala in September 2010 was, for the first time in the preservation era, an impressive quartet of locomotives built for the London & South Western Railway, all of which were in steam and working trains. Visiting from the Swanage Railway was 'M7' Class 0-4-4T No 53 (BR No 30053), which, although built in 1905, was the youngest of the quartet! Designed by Dugald Drummond, the 'M7' Class totalled 105 locomotives built between 1897 and 1911. In later years many members of the class became a regular sight on branch lines in Southern England, including the Plymouth area. No 53 makes an impressive sight climbing towards Bridge 7 on 4 September 2010. *Graham Hutton*

Above **THREE ARCH BRIDGE:** Bridge 8, or Three Arch Bridge, carries the A38 trunk road over the line. GWR '4575' Class 2-6-2T No 5552 looks very much at home as it bursts under the impressive structure with a train bound for Bodmin General on 10 April 2005. Members of the class were a very regular sight on both passenger and goods trains on the Bodmin branch for more than 40 years, based at St Blazey shed (SBZ, 83E, 84B). *Mike Tyack*

Left **QUARRY CURVE:** The line from Bodmin Parkway to Bodmin General climbs sharply, on gradients as steep as 1 in 37, for 2½ miles before reaching the summit at 'Quarry Curve', near Bridge 11, then descending on more gentle gradients to reach the branch terminus. Visiting English Electric Type 4 diesel locomotive (later Class 50) No D449 passes the summit on 31 March 2001 with a train bound for Bodmin General. *Brian Aston*

Right **QUARRY CURVE:** Seen looking the other way from Bridge 11, and having cleared the speed restriction over the point giving entry to Walker Lines Sidings, GWR '42xx' Class 2-8-0T No 4247 accelerates away with the 12.10pm Bodmin General to Bodmin Parkway train on 9 April 2010. Note the very tidy and well-kept lineside. In the background the Gilbert Monument dominates the skyline as it stands on Bodmin Beacon. *Richard Jones*

Below **Nr QUARRY CURVE:** A pair of panniers! No 6435 leads No 4612 as they double-head a train from Bodmin Parkway to Bodmin General on the straight approaching Quarry Curve on 19 April 2009. Both these Great Western pannier tanks are regulars in the railway's steam fleet, and very popular with visitors and enginemen alike. *Audrey Mills*

COMMERCIAL FREIGHT TRAFFIC:
The Bodmin & Wenford Railway is one of a very few heritage lines to have carried commercial freight traffic, when a local company, Fitzgerald Lighting, decided to use rail to move its products using a siding adjacent to its factory on the industrial estate at Walker Lines, approximately three-quarters of a mile from Bodmin General station. The freight was moved by a BWR locomotive to and from the 'Exchange Siding' at Bodmin Parkway, where a main-line diesel took over. The Fitzgerald freight traffic ran from December 1989 to July 1991 as part of BR's Railfreight Distribution network, and again between September 1996 and July 2001 after rail privatisation, but proved to be uneconomic.

Top left **WALKER LINES:** Class 33 diesel No 33110 awaits departure from Walker Lines Sidings on 25 June 2001 with two loaded wagons of lighting products bound for the North of England. *Brian Aston*

Left **Nr QUARRY CURVE:** The railway's Class 10 diesel shunter, No D3452 – which spent most of its working life shunting clay trains at Fowey Docks under the ownership of English China Clays – drifts downhill towards Bodmin Parkway with three loaded wagons and a brake-van in tow on 17 June 1992. *Brian Aston*

Top right **BODMIN PARKWAY:** During the time when main-line freight operator EWS (English Welsh & Scottish Railway Co) worked the freight traffic, the then relatively new pairing of Class 67 No 67008 and Class 66 No 66161 wait in the 'Exchange Siding' at Bodmin Parkway on 7 October 2000. With funding generously provided by the BWR Trust, in 2007 a new carriage shed was later built over the sidings behind the train, an invaluable asset in keeping rolling stock under cover. *Brian Aston*

Below **BODMIN GENERAL:** A superb view of Bodmin Station circa 1890, with people suitably posed for the occasion! At that time the railway had been opened for less than five years. The main station building can be clearly seen, while to the left is the corner of the former goods shed. The former Weighbridge Office and cattle dock can just be glimpsed through the group of people to the right. Also worthy of note are the steps between the platform and Harleigh Road, the green fields in the background, and the total absence of houses. The station did not receive the suffix 'General' until 1949. *Maurice Dart collection*

Above **BODMIN GENERAL:** A slightly later view shows railway staff posing for the camera beside the branch passenger train, hauled by a '517' Class 0-4-2 tank locomotive. Worthy of mention are the very tidy appearance of the platform and the adjacent bank, the diamond-chequered bricks forming the platform surface, and the position of the gas lamps. *Maurice Dart Collection*

Below **BODMIN GENERAL** is bathed in a light covering of snow on 25 November 2010. *Richard Jones*

Right **BODMIN GENERAL:** In this view of the station forecourt and approach in the early British Railways era, note the interesting collection of vehicles, including a Western National bus. Harleigh Road can be seen to the right and the barracks (now Cornwall's Regimental Museum) in the left background. *Maurice Dart Collection*

Below right **BODMIN GENERAL:** The station is now the Head Office and principal station of the Bodmin & Wenford Railway, and welcomes well in excess of 50,000 visitors a year. The platform area around the main buffer stops is viewed on a bright and sunny early morning, well before visitors arrive for the day. *Ben Harding*

Left **BODMIN GENERAL:** An impressive steam quintet line-up is berthed on the 'Shed Road' at Bodmin General on 19 April 2009. From left to right, the locomotives in view are the pair of Bagnall 0-4-0STs *Alfred* and *Judy*, LSWR Beattie 2-4-0WT No 30587, GWR '64xx' Class 0-6-0PT No 6435, and GWR '8750' Class 0-6-0PT No 4612. All five engines are based on the line, although the Beattie well tank is owned by the National Railway Museum and on long-term loan to the BWR. In the background can be seen the railway's workshop, the construction of which was one of the first major tasks undertaken after the line was secured for preservation. The impressive-looking building that dominates the background is now Cornwall's Regimental Museum. *Audrey Mills*

Below left **BODMIN GENERAL:** The BWR has been used for a number of filming assignments over the years. On one such occasion, on 8 May 2009, a German television crew film the arrival of No 4247 from the platform. *Richard Jones*

Left **BODMIN GENERAL:** The BWR stages a wide range of special events during the course of each year, to suit a wide range of ages and interests. The Heritage Transport Festival, introduced in 2010 and taking place in mid-June, has rapidly become one of its most popular such events. An impressive array of road and rail transport exhibits is seen on display at Bodmin General on 20 June 2010. *Richard Jones*

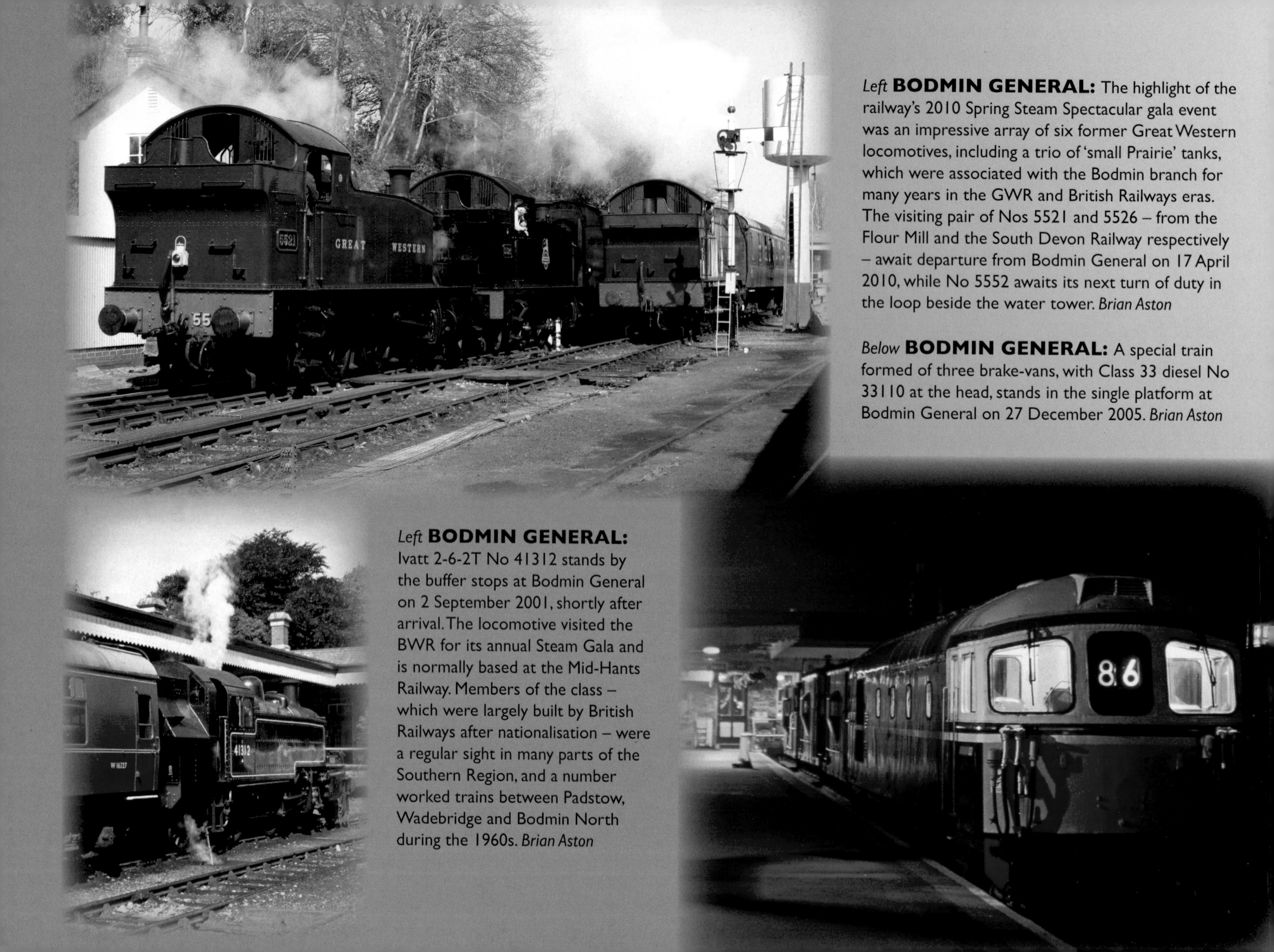

Left **BODMIN GENERAL:** The highlight of the railway's 2010 Spring Steam Spectacular gala event was an impressive array of six former Great Western locomotives, including a trio of 'small Prairie' tanks, which were associated with the Bodmin branch for many years in the GWR and British Railways eras. The visiting pair of Nos 5521 and 5526 – from the Flour Mill and the South Devon Railway respectively – await departure from Bodmin General on 17 April 2010, while No 5552 awaits its next turn of duty in the loop beside the water tower. *Brian Aston*

Below **BODMIN GENERAL:** A special train formed of three brake-vans, with Class 33 diesel No 33110 at the head, stands in the single platform at Bodmin General on 27 December 2005. *Brian Aston*

Left **BODMIN GENERAL:** Ivatt 2-6-2T No 41312 stands by the buffer stops at Bodmin General on 2 September 2001, shortly after arrival. The locomotive visited the BWR for its annual Steam Gala and is normally based at the Mid-Hants Railway. Members of the class – which were largely built by British Railways after nationalisation – were a regular sight in many parts of the Southern Region, and a number worked trains between Padstow, Wadebridge and Bodmin North during the 1960s. *Brian Aston*

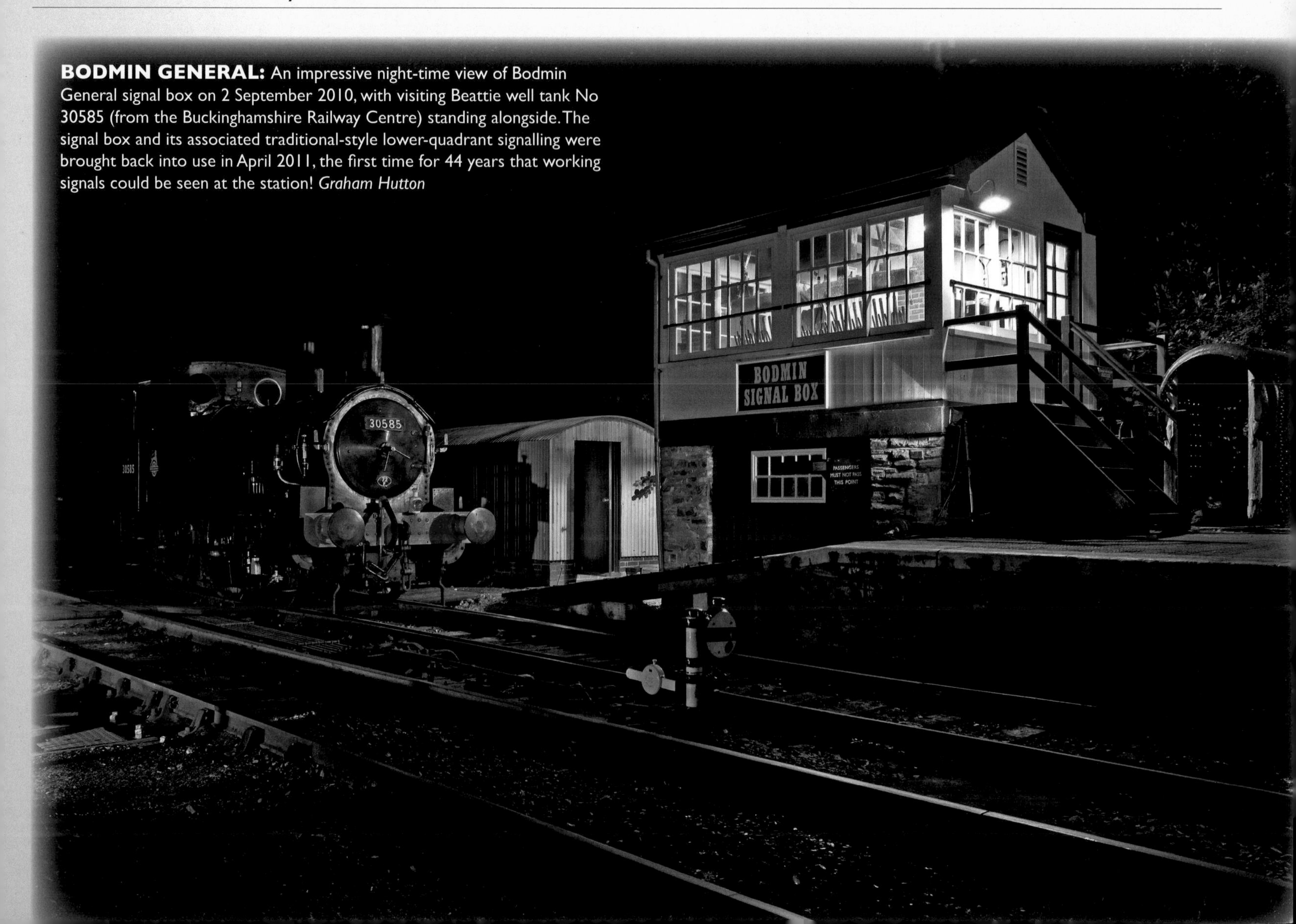

BODMIN GENERAL: An impressive night-time view of Bodmin General signal box on 2 September 2010, with visiting Beattie well tank No 30585 (from the Buckinghamshire Railway Centre) standing alongside. The signal box and its associated traditional-style lower-quadrant signalling were brought back into use in April 2011, the first time for 44 years that working signals could be seen at the station! *Graham Hutton*

Above left **BODMIN GENERAL** once had a single-road stone-built engine shed, a sub-shed of St Blazey and sufficient to stable the branch locomotive – normally a '45xx' or '4575' Class 2-6-2T – overnight. Three sets of enginemen were based here until the shed was closed by British Railways in 1962. The South West Group of the Great Western Society was based here for a number of years from 1969 and occupied the disused shed, where its GWR '1361' Class 0-6-0ST No 1363 was based. Sadly, BR demolished the shed in about 1974, though the inspection pits remained in situ. In this fascinating view inside the shed note the wooden wheelbarrow and gas lighting. *Maurice Dart Collection*

Above right **BODMIN GENERAL:** The Bodmin & Wenford Railway later excavated the old pits, over which was built a new two-road shed in 1991, extended two years later. Known as the 'Locomotive Running Shed', it enables the line's impressive fleet of steam engines to be stored, and prepared for duty, under cover and away from the worst of the Cornish weather! Memories of Wadebridge shed in the 1950s are evoked in this view of GWR 'small Prairie' No 5552 and LSWR 'T9' 4-4-0 No 30120 awaiting their next turn of duty on 2 September 2010. *Brian Aston*

Left **BODMIN GENERAL:** The GWR 'small Prairie' tank pairing of Nos 5521 and 5526 departs from Bodmin General with the 12.20pm train to Bodmin Parkway on 17 April 2010. Both locomotives were shedded at St Blazey for part of their working lives on the GWR and BR, and would thus have worked trains between Bodmin Road and Wadebridge/Padstow. *Dave Letcher*

Right **FORMER LSWR LOCOMOTIVES:** A very impressive line-up of three former London & South Western Railway locomotives – all of which were associated with the former North Cornwall and Wenfordbridge lines – is seen on shed at Bodmin General on 2 September 2010. To the left can be seen the only surviving member of the 'T9' Class, No 30120, owned by the National Railway Museum. After 18 years out of use, the locomotive received an extensive overhaul in 2008-10, generously funded by the BWR Trust, and is now based on the line. On the two shed roads are the unique pair of Beattie well tanks, Nos 30587 and 30585, which – together with sister engine No 30586 – were based at nearby Wadebridge shed for more than 60 years. No 30587 is the oldest steam locomotive currently on the line, having been built in 1874. *Andrew Dennison*

Above At the end of a long day, the crew of No 30120 begin disposing their locomotive on shed at Bodmin General on 21 October 2010. *Brian Aston*

Left **BODMIN GENERAL SHED:** No 6435 shunts two other former Great Western engines, Nos 4612 and 4247, into the Locomotive Running Shed on 8 August 2009. Although all three engines are painted Brunswick green, the three different livery variations are of particular note. *Brian Aston*

Below **BODMIN GENERAL:** GWR '45xx' 2-6-2T No 4559 departs from Bodmin General on 2 June 1960 with a train for Wadebridge and Padstow. The train is formed of a two-coach 'B set', which was the regular branch passenger train formation for many years. This view gives a good general view of the station area and the various buildings, and of particular note is the very smart and well-kept lineside. *Colour-Rail.com*

Right **BODMIN GENERAL:** Looking across from above the engine shed, another GWR 'small Prairie' tank, No 4569, stands with another 'B set' on the goods shed road awaiting its next turn of duty on 9 June 1956. Visible in the background is the goods shed, the 6-ton-capacity yard crane and an agricultural merchant's store. *Maurice Dart Collection*

Below **BODMIN GENERAL:** LSWR Beattie 2-4-0WT No 30587 shunts wagons at Boscarne Junction on 27 August 1962 before working a train down the Wenfordbridge branch. Ironically, No 30587 can still be seen working trains at Boscarne to this day, as the locomotive is a member of the steam fleet based at Bodmin, having returned to steam after overhaul in 2002. *Colour-Rail.com*

BOSCARNE JUNCTION: This excellent view of Boscarne Junction was taken from the top of the bracket signal in December 1966, with the signal box and railway cottage in the foreground. A rake of china clay wagons can be seen stabled in one of the two 'sidings', adjacent to which is the 'Southern' route to Bodmin North and Wenfordbridge (which diverged a little further beyond at Dunmere Junction). On the far right is the 'Western' line to Bodmin General, the two lines converging at the points in the foreground to become the single line to Wadebridge. *Bernard Mills*

Above **BODMIN GENERAL:** BR Class 37 diesel No 37299 heads away from a rather desolate-looking Bodmin General on 13 May 1982 with a rake of 'clay hoods' bound for Boscarne Junction and, ultimately, the clay dries at Wenfordbridge. Passenger services over the line ceased on 30 January 1967, but the station signal box remained in use until 17 December of that year. Compare the general appearance of the station area in this view with the photograph (on page 28) of No 4559 some 20 or so years earlier. *Brian Aston*

A wide variety of visiting locomotives, both steam and diesel, have graced the Bodmin & Wenford Railway in its 25-year history as a heritage line, many of which would certainly not have appeared on a Cornish branch line in GWR or BR days. Many locomotives were hired for a particular special event, while others have spent a whole summer season on the line.

Above **BRIDGE 8:** Evoking memories of the days when the Great Western 'small prairie' tanks were a very regular sight on the branch, the 1924-built No 4561 – a former St Blazey engine – passes Three Arch Bridge (Bridge 8) on 4 September 1996 as it heads for Bodmin General. No 4561 was rescued from Barry scrapyard for preservation in 1975 and has been based on the West Somerset Railway ever since. *Brian Aston*

Above **COLESLOGGETT HALT:** Undoubtedly the heaviest steam locomotive to have ever traversed the route was GWR 'King' 4-6-0 No 6024 *King Edward I* in 1998. In GWR and BR days 'King' Class locomotives were not permitted to traverse Brunel's Royal Albert Bridge over the River Tamar, and thus were not seen in Cornwall. A family watches from the safety of the platform at Colesloggett Halt as No 6024 heads up the gradient with a train for Bodmin General. *Audrey Mills*

Right **BODMIN PARKWAY:** GWR '2251' Class 0-6-0 No 3205 – then based on the West Somerset Railway – was a very popular visitor to the line for the 1997 Steam Gala, and is seen here departing from Bodmin Parkway with a short demonstration goods train on 6 September of that year. Note the typical GWR 'Toad' brake-van on the left and the GWR 'Siphon G' bogie van stabled adjacent to the main-line platform to the right. No 3205 – the only preserved member of its class – is now based on the South Devon Railway. *Brian Aston*

DIESELS ON TOUR: This colourful selection of images shows some of the visiting diesel locomotives that have worked over the Bodmin branch in the preservation era, principally at special events such as Diesel Galas.

Above **CHARLIE'S GATE:** Class 35 'Hymek' No D7017 – normally based on the West Somerset Railway – passes Charlie's Gate with a train bound for Bodmin Parkway on 5 October 1991. *Brian Aston*

Left **BODMIN PARKWAY:** In BR Civil Engineers' 'Dutch' livery, Class 31 No 31273 arrives at Bodmin Parkway on 20 September 1997. *Brian Aston*

Top right **BODMIN GENERAL:** A trio of Class 47s meet at Bodmin General during the 2008 Spring Diesel Gala. On the left are Nos 47727 *Rebecca* and 47749 *Damelza*, both resplendent in the house colours of Colas Rail, while BWR-based No 47306 *The Sapper* (formerly No D1787) can be seen on the right. *Richard Jones*

Above **BODMIN GENERAL:** Another Class 47, No 47736 *Cambridge Traction and Rolling Stock Maintenance Depot* – with Class 20 No 20166 tucked inside – makes a smoky departure from Bodmin General in October 1999. The Brush/Sulzer Type 4 locomotive – here seen in Rail Express Systems livery – was built in 1965 as No D1963, and was withdrawn from service in 2004. *Brian Aston*

Above **BODMIN PARKWAY:** Visiting from nearby St Blazey, courtesy of English Welsh & Scottish Railway (EWS), the then new Class 66 No 66125 is seen on display at the end of the 'Shed Road' at Bodmin General with a pair of air-braked 'CDA' china clay wagons on 4 October 1999. *Brian Aston*

Right **QUARRY CURVE:** EWS Class 37 No 37406 – an English Electric Type 3 locomotive built originally for British Railways in 1965 as No D6995 – crests the highest point of the line at 'Quarry Curve' on 21 September 2002 with a train for Bodmin Parkway. *Brian Aston*

Above **BOSCARNE JUNCTION:** Recalling its days working the Wenfordbridge branch, LSWR Beattie well tank No 30585 makes a delightful image as it heads away from Boscarne Junction with a demonstration china clay train on 5 September 2010. *Andrew Dennison*

Below **QUARRY CURVE:** Visiting GWR '4575' Class 2-6-2T No 5553 – built at Swindon in 1928 and withdrawn by British Railways in 1961– looks very much at home on the line as it rounds 'Quarry Curve' on 26 October 2008 heading for Bodmin General. Its last year in service with BR was spent in Cornwall, largely based at St Blazey, and it worked the branch trains between Bodmin Road and Wadebridge/Padstow during this time. Now owned by the Waterman Heritage Railway Trust, No 5553 was the very last of 212 steam locomotives rescued for preservation from Woodham's scrapyard at Barry in South Wales. *Richard Jones*

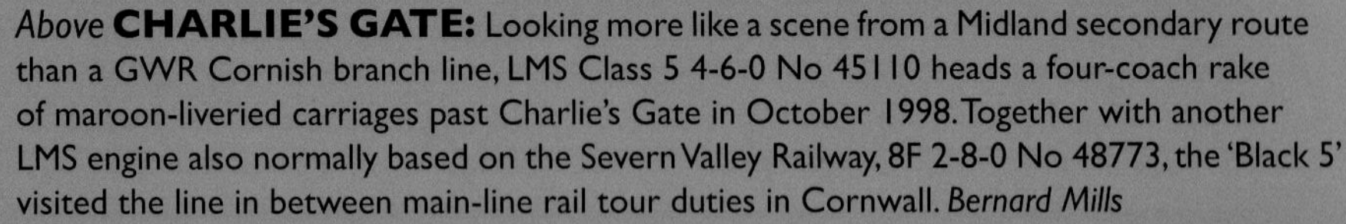
Above **CHARLIE'S GATE:** Looking more like a scene from a Midland secondary route than a GWR Cornish branch line, LMS Class 5 4-6-0 No 45110 heads a four-coach rake of maroon-liveried carriages past Charlie's Gate in October 1998. Together with another LMS engine also normally based on the Severn Valley Railway, 8F 2-8-0 No 48773, the 'Black 5' visited the line in between main-line rail tour duties in Cornwall. *Bernard Mills*

Above right **WEST HEATH ROAD:** Amidst a carpet of wild flowers, GWR '4575' Class 2-6-2T No 5521 climbs the gradient past West Heath Road on 16 April 2010 with the 12.53pm train from Boscarne Junction to Bodmin General, during the railway's Spring Steam Spectacular event. No 5521 is one of seven Great Western 'small Prairie' tanks to have worked over the Bodmin & Wenford Railway in the preservation era, the others being Nos 4561, 5526, 5541, 5542, 5552 and 5553. *Bernard Mills*

Right **BODMIN GENERAL:** Another GWR 'small Prairie' tank, No 5542 – unusually facing 'the other way round' – departs from Bodmin General with an auto-train (formed of 1930-built trailer No 178) bound for Boscarne Junction on 1 May 2004. Compare this view with the images taken from a similar position on pages 28 and 30. *Brian Aston*

The 3-mile branch between Bodmin and Boscarne Junction, which also has steep gradients and sharp curves, was built by the Great Western Railway and opened on 3 September 1888, to connect with the original Bodmin & Wadebridge Railway, which had opened in 1834. This meant that the china clay traffic from Wenford could be conveyed via the GWR instead of the inadequate wharves in Wadebridge. Following closure of the line by British Railways in 1983, trains started running to Boscarne Junction again in 1996.

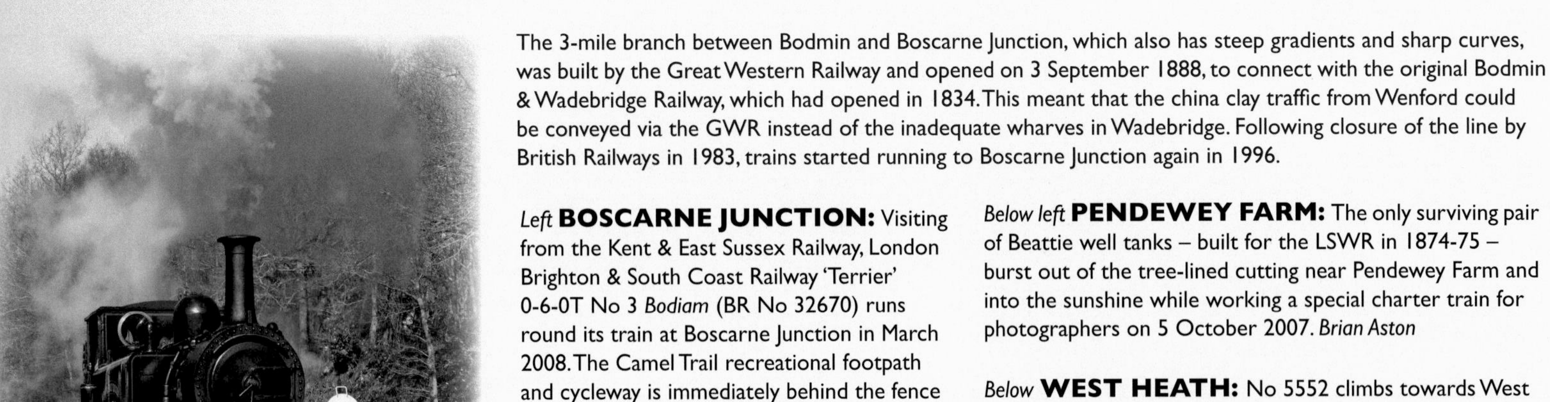

Left **BOSCARNE JUNCTION:** Visiting from the Kent & East Sussex Railway, London Brighton & South Coast Railway 'Terrier' 0-6-0T No 3 *Bodiam* (BR No 32670) runs round its train at Boscarne Junction in March 2008. The Camel Trail recreational footpath and cycleway is immediately behind the fence in the background. *Dave Letcher*

Below left **PENDEWEY FARM:** The only surviving pair of Beattie well tanks – built for the LSWR in 1874-75 – burst out of the tree-lined cutting near Pendewey Farm and into the sunshine while working a special charter train for photographers on 5 October 2007. *Brian Aston*

Below **WEST HEATH:** No 5552 climbs towards West Heath Road and past the western outskirts of Bodmin as it heads for Bodmin General with a three-coach train on 27 December 2008. *Audrey Mills*

Above **WEST HEATH ROAD:** In this very colourful spring scene at West Heath Road, a typical 1950s British Railways Western Region auto-train – formed of '64xx' Class 0-6-0PT No 6435 and trailer W232W, both of which are based on the line – heads towards Bodmin General with a special charter working on 10 May 2011. *Peter Zabek*

Above right **WEST HEATH ROAD:** Shades of early autumn, as the beautifully restored London & South Western Railway pairing of Beattie 2-4-0 well tank No 30585 and 'T9' Class 4-4-0 No 30120, with a smart rake of four BR carmine-and-cream-liveried Mark 1 carriages in tow, works an afternoon passenger train from Boscarne Junction to Bodmin General during the railway's Branch Line Weekend on 10 October 2010 (10.10.10!). *Graham Hutton*

Below **Nr BODMIN BEACON:** Steam in the landscape – Bodmin-based Great Western Railway 'small Prairie' tank No 5552 – which has spent virtually all its working life in the West Country – climbs the gradient towards Bodmin General in December 2009. Bodmin Beacon dominates the background, on which sits the Gilbert Monument, 144 feet high and erected in 1857 as a memorial to Walter Raleigh Gilbert, a descendant of Sir Walter Raleigh. Born in Bodmin in 1785, Gilbert received a baronetcy from Queen Victoria in 1851 for his distinguished military service. *Sam Felce*

Left **'BRIDGE 16':** The daffodils are in bloom as GWR '57xx' 0-6-0PT No 4612 drifts downhill over Bridge 16 on 15 March 2009, heading for Boscarne Junction. The '57xx' Class of pannier tanks constituted the largest single group of locomotives on the GWR, with a total of 863 built between 1929 and 1950. After complete restoration from scrapyard condition, which involved the replacement of many missing parts, No 4612 became the first of the railway's own ex-BR engines to return to steam on the line, in 2001. *Audrey Mills*

Below left **CRABTREE LANE:** With the beautiful Cornish countryside in the background, two locomotives in the Bodmin-based steam fleet, Nos 30587 and 4612, climb towards Bodmin General and past Crabtree Lane (Bridge 15) on 17 April 2009. Built in 1874, and now owned by the National Railway Museum and on long-term loan to the BWR, the Beattie well tank is 'our' oldest locomotive, while the 1942-built No 4612 is the newest member of the steam fleet! *Audrey Mills*

Right **Nr HALGAVOR ROAD:** With a light covering of snow on the ground, LSWR 'T9' Class 4-4-0 No 30120 catches the winter sunlight as it passes Bodmin General's Up Branch Fixed Distant signal on 18 December 2010, hauling one of the railway's extremely popular 'Santa by Steam' trains that run each year. *Dave Letcher*

Above **'CHECK RAIL CURVE':** Evoking memories of the steam era on the nearby Lostwithiel-Fowey branch – where such trains were once a very regular sight – the auto-train pairing of GWR '14xx' Class 0-4-2T No 1450 and trailer W228W heads around 'Check Rail Curve' on the approach to Bodmin General on 10 May 1997. No 1450 normally works on the Dean Forest Railway, while No W228W is based at Buckfastleigh, one of five ex-BR(W) auto-trailers (including the BWR's own No W232W) originally purchased for preservation in the mid-1960s by the Dart Valley Railway. *Brian Aston*

A NEW ERA: Not long after British Rail finally closed the line from Bodmin Road to Wenfordbridge (via Bodmin General and Boscarne Junction) in September 1983 – having been used solely by freight traffic since passenger services ceased in January 1967 – efforts began to examine the possibility of the line being purchased from BR and re-opened as 'Cornwall's only standard gauge steam railway'. As a result, the Bodmin Railway Preservation Society (BRPS) was formed in July 1984 and, subsequently, the Bodmin & Wenford Railway plc the following year. Following a successful share issue, the company purchased the 6½ miles of track between Bodmin Road and Boscarne Junction, with the (then) North Cornwall District Council securing the land from BR. A new era had begun for the Bodmin branch...

Above **BODMIN GENERAL:** This interesting view shows the station area at Bodmin General from the 'buffer stops end' in 1986. Some of the early items of rolling stock secured for preservation on the line can be seen, including, in the right foreground, GWR 2-6-2T No 5552 in 'as bought scrapyard condition'. The 'new' workshop building is being erected in the background, while on the left is one of the German-built AC railbuses, No W79976, which is now no longer on the line. A far cry from the scene of today... *Keith Searle*

The majority of trains in the early years of the Bodmin & Wenford Railway were worked by a small fleet of former industrial locomotives, which was all the line had at the time!

Right **BODMIN GENERAL:** One of the former 'Port of Par' pair of Bagnall saddle tanks, *Alfred*, has been based on the BWR since 1987. The locomotive worked several of the first trips on the line during the preservation era and is here seen giving brake-van rides from the single platform at Bodmin General, in the company of three long-serving volunteers – Lyn Davies, the late Alan Allday and Keith Searle. *Keith Searle Collection*

Far right top **CHARLIE'S GATE:** With the shadows lengthening, RSH 0-6-0T No 7597 passes Charlie's Gate in the late afternoon with an early 'Santa Special' train bound for Bodmin General. The locomotive was built by Robert Stephenson & Hawthorn at Newcastle in 1949 and worked in various power stations in Hertfordshire in 1971, when it was purchased for preservation. No 7597 was based at Bodmin from 1993 to 2001. *Audrey Mills*

Inset right **COLESLOGGETT HALT:** One of the ubiquitous 'Austerity' 0-6-0 saddle tanks, No 2857 *Swiftsure* – in a very smart blue livery – climbs away from Colesloggett Halt. Built by Hunslet in 1943, *Swiftsure* was one of 484 locomotives built for use by the War Department during the Second World War. During its WD service it was given the number 75008 and worked in Belgium. After the war it returned to Britain and worked in the Yorkshire coalfields. *Swiftsure* was purchased for preservation at the BWR in 1987 and was a mainstay of the steam fleet for almost 20 years. *Bernard Mills*

Right **Nr QUARRY CURVE:** With a four-coach rake in tow, Robert Stephenson & Hawthorn 0-6-0ST No 62 *Ugly* heads along the straight towards 'Quarry Curve'. Built in 1950 for use on the various ironstone branches near Corby, it was originally fitted with electric headlights and painted unlined green. Initially purchased for preservation at the Keighley & Worth Valley Railway, No 62 arrived at Bodmin in 1990 and worked on the line until 2002. *Audrey Mills*

Below **DREASON:** The railway's two ex-BR diesel shunting locomotives are frequently seen on shunting and works train duties, but very rarely on passenger trains. During a Diesel Gala Weekend Class 10 No D3452 and Class 08 No D3559 – in BR black and later BR green respectively – make an interesting sight at Dreason, near Bodmin Parkway, on 5 October 1991. Built more than 50 years ago, such shunters were once a very common sight throughout the country, and several are still active on such duties today. No D3559 was built at Derby in 1958, while the Class 10 is a year older (1957, Darlington) and spent most of its working life shunting clay trains at nearby Fowey Docks. *Brian Aston*

Right **BODMIN PARKWAY:** Two years after passenger trains started running regular timetabled passenger services, the railway was very fortunate to be able to hire the record-breaking steam locomotive *City of Truro*. A real icon of the Victorian steam age, the locomotive – owned by the National Railway Museum – spent the 1992 summer season working trains on the line and proved very popular. Passengers clamour for a closer look as the 1903-built engine awaits departure from Bodmin Parkway on 30 May 1992. *Brian Aston*

Below **BOSCARNE JUNCTION:** In the days before regular trains began operating again over the Boscarne branch, GWR '57xx' 0-6-0PT No 7752 stands at Boscarne Junction with a special photographers' charter train on 5 September 1994. No 7752 was built for the Great Western by the North British Locomotive Co Ltd in Glasgow in 1930. After spending all its working life with the GWR and British Railways working in South Wales, the locomotive was sold – together with several other pannier tanks from the same class – to London Transport for use on engineers' trains. No 7752 hauled the very last steam train on 'The Met' on 6 June 1971, and is now one of three '57xx' Class engines based at Tyseley Locomotive Works in Birmingham. *Brian Aston*

ST BLAZEY SHED: During the Great Western Railway and British Railways eras the locomotives that worked on the Bodmin branch were provided by St Blazey shed, although a sub-shed was provided at Bodmin from 1887 until 1962. St Blazey shed is of Cornwall Minerals Railway origin and dates from circa 1872. Its unique feature was a nine-road semi-roundhouse, which survived long into the diesel era. In later years the majority of the allocation at St Blazey shed (SBZ, later 83E, then 84B) comprised ex-GWR '45xx'/'4575' and '57xx' Class locomotives.

Right **ST BLAZEY:** One of the BWR's current steam locomotive fleet, GWR 2-8-0T No 4247, was a St Blazey engine with British Railways between November 1952 and January 1958, when it was largely deployed to work the heavy china clay trains down to the docks at Fowey. St Blazey normally had a pair of these '42xx' Class tanks for such work. No 4247 is seen stabled at the shed on 23 April 1956. *Colour-Rail.com*

Below and below right **ST BLAZEY:** Three BWR-based locomotives paid a visit to St Blazey Depot on 31 August 2002 for a special staff Open Day. No 33110 is seen outside the shed in the company of privately owned Class 52 'Western' No D1015 *Western Champion*, while Bagnall 0-4-0ST *Alfred* stands on the turntable (with EWS Class 60 No 60031 in the background), a short distance from the place it worked for so many years. *Brian Aston*

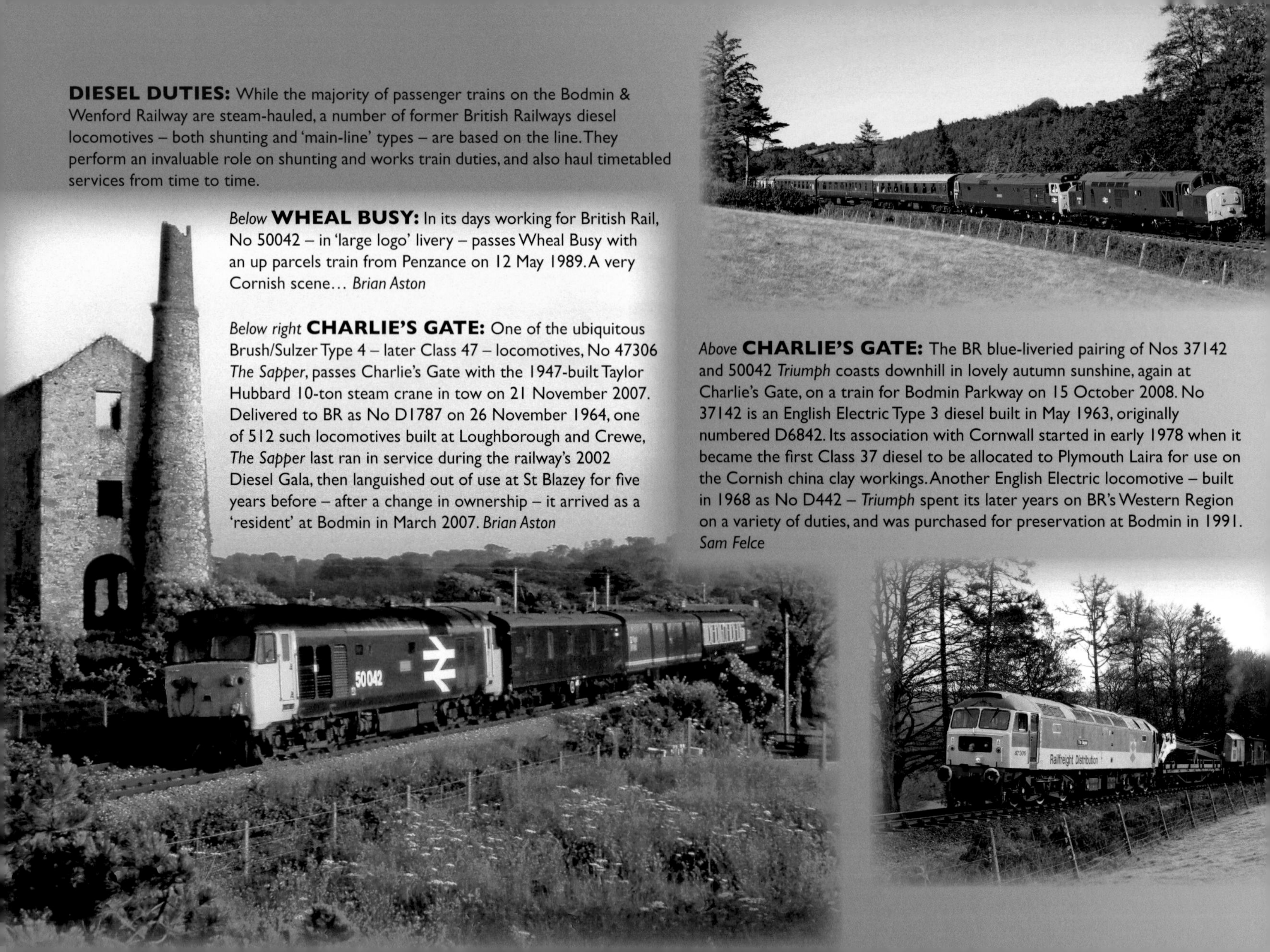

DIESEL DUTIES: While the majority of passenger trains on the Bodmin & Wenford Railway are steam-hauled, a number of former British Railways diesel locomotives – both shunting and 'main-line' types – are based on the line. They perform an invaluable role on shunting and works train duties, and also haul timetabled services from time to time.

Below **WHEAL BUSY:** In its days working for British Rail, No 50042 – in 'large logo' livery – passes Wheal Busy with an up parcels train from Penzance on 12 May 1989. A very Cornish scene… *Brian Aston*

Below right **CHARLIE'S GATE:** One of the ubiquitous Brush/Sulzer Type 4 – later Class 47 – locomotives, No 47306 *The Sapper*, passes Charlie's Gate with the 1947-built Taylor Hubbard 10-ton steam crane in tow on 21 November 2007. Delivered to BR as No D1787 on 26 November 1964, one of 512 such locomotives built at Loughborough and Crewe, *The Sapper* last ran in service during the railway's 2002 Diesel Gala, then languished out of use at St Blazey for five years before – after a change in ownership – it arrived as a 'resident' at Bodmin in March 2007. *Brian Aston*

Above **CHARLIE'S GATE:** The BR blue-liveried pairing of Nos 37142 and 50042 *Triumph* coasts downhill in lovely autumn sunshine, again at Charlie's Gate, on a train for Bodmin Parkway on 15 October 2008. No 37142 is an English Electric Type 3 diesel built in May 1963, originally numbered D6842. Its association with Cornwall started in early 1978 when it became the first Class 37 diesel to be allocated to Plymouth Laira for use on the Cornish china clay workings. Another English Electric locomotive – built in 1968 as No D442 – *Triumph* spent its later years on BR's Western Region on a variety of duties, and was purchased for preservation at Bodmin in 1991. *Sam Felce*

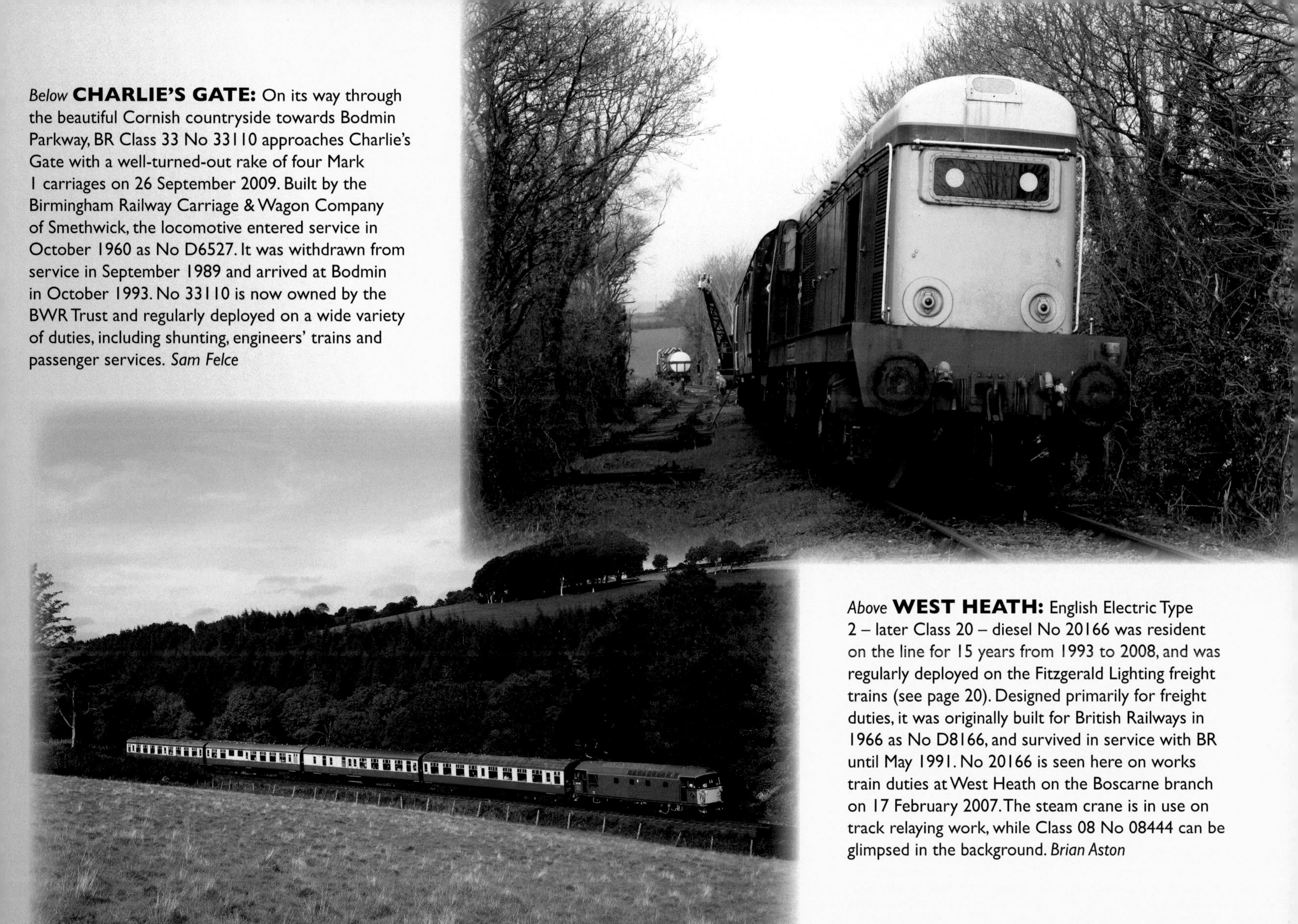

Below **CHARLIE'S GATE:** On its way through the beautiful Cornish countryside towards Bodmin Parkway, BR Class 33 No 33110 approaches Charlie's Gate with a well-turned-out rake of four Mark 1 carriages on 26 September 2009. Built by the Birmingham Railway Carriage & Wagon Company of Smethwick, the locomotive entered service in October 1960 as No D6527. It was withdrawn from service in September 1989 and arrived at Bodmin in October 1993. No 33110 is now owned by the BWR Trust and regularly deployed on a wide variety of duties, including shunting, engineers' trains and passenger services. *Sam Felce*

Above **WEST HEATH:** English Electric Type 2 – later Class 20 – diesel No 20166 was resident on the line for 15 years from 1993 to 2008, and was regularly deployed on the Fitzgerald Lighting freight trains (see page 20). Designed primarily for freight duties, it was originally built for British Railways in 1966 as No D8166, and survived in service with BR until May 1991. No 20166 is seen here on works train duties at West Heath on the Boscarne branch on 17 February 2007. The steam crane is in use on track relaying work, while Class 08 No 08444 can be glimpsed in the background. *Brian Aston*

Right **BOSCARNE JUNCTION:** The Class 42/43 'Warship' diesel-hydraulic locomotives were once a regular sight with British Rail on the main line through Cornwall, but were not seen on the Bodmin branch. One of the two surviving locomotives, No D821 *Greyhound* – a regular Plymouth Laira engine for most of its working life, and now normally based on the Severn Valley Railway – became the first 'Warship' to work on the line. It is seen here on 31 March 2001 shortly after arrival at Boscarne Junction with a mixed rake of maroon Mark 1 and early Mark 2 coaches. *Brian Aston*

Above **BOSCARNE JUNCTION:** Another Severn Valley-based engine, BR(W) '15xx' Class 0-6-0PT No 1501 awaits departure from Boscarne on 1 September 1998. Designed by the last Chief Mechanical Engineer of the Great Western Railway, F.W. Hawksworth, ten locomotives in the '15xx' Class were built in 1949, primarily for shunting duties. Several members of the class were regularly deployed on empty coaching stock duties between Old Oak Common shed and London Paddington. With its outside cylinders and high tractive effort, No 1501 proved itself to be ideally suited to working trains at relatively low speeds over the BWR's steep gradients. *Brian Aston*

Above **BOSCARNE JUNCTION:** Looking 'up grade', the double-headed pairing of LSWR Beattie 2-4-0WT No 30587 and GWR '57xx' Class 0-6-0PT No 4612 awaits departure back to Bodmin General on 5 April 2009. Both locomotives are based at Bodmin, owned by the BWR Trust and the National Railway Museum respectively. The former Southern line to Bodmin North and Wenfordbridge, which is now the Camel Trail recreational footpath and cycleway, can be glimpsed above the buffer beam of No 30587. *Richard Jones*

Above **BOSCARNE JUNCTION:** Recreating the days when the Beattie well tanks were a regular sight on china clay trains to Wenfordbridge, the unique pairing of Nos 30585 and 30587 departs from Boscarne Junction with a special photographers' charter train on 5 October 2007. *Brian Aston*

Right **BOSCARNE JUNCTION:** The station here was built by the Bodmin & Wenford Railway and opened in August 1996. The platform itself occupies the site of the former Southern line (see the photograph on page 29), and sits directly adjacent to the Camel Trail, which offers passengers a chance to break their journey, perhaps for a gentle stroll or a pub lunch! The station was further enhanced by a new platform waiting room, funded by the Bodmin Railway Preservation Society, which was officially opened on 16 September 2009. A group of local dignitaries line up for the camera prior to the traditional ribbon-cutting ceremony. *Don Bishop, Richard Jones*

Above **Nr BOSCARNE JUNCTION:** Very shortly after departure from Boscarne Junction, the railway's two-car Class 108 diesel multiple unit crosses Bridge 24 – which carries the line over the River Camel below – on 16 September 2009. Once a regular sight on many West Country branch lines, the DMU now performs a valuable support role on the BWR. *Brian Aston*

Below **Nr BOSCARNE:** Masquerading as scrapped sister engine No 4666, GWR 0-6-0PT No 4612 makes a brisk departure from Boscarne with a demonstration china clay train on 10 October 2010. After nine years in GWR green livery following restoration, No 4612 was repainted in BR unlined black that autumn for the last few months of its boiler ticket, much to the delight of photographers! No 4666 was one of a trio of pannier tanks sent by BR Western Region to Wadebridge shed in 1962, primarily to displace the LSWR 'O2' Class 0-4-4 tanks. *Brian Aston*

Left **Nr BOSCARNE:** LSWR 'T9' 4-4-0 No 30120 – obtained for preservation in 1962, owned by the National Railway Museum and on long-term loan to the Bodmin & Wenford Railway – climbs away from the River Camel at Boscarne with a special charter train working on 22 October 2010. *Martin Creese*

During the steam era, Boscarne Junction was once a busy centre of railway activity, with trains serving Bodmin (General), Bodmin Road, Bodmin North, Wenfordbridge, Wadebridge and Padstow, operated by both the 'Western' and the 'Southern', and worked by a variety of different classes of locomotive. The photographs on this and the next pages depict a selection of 'what might have been' images – and, who knows, perhaps a snapshot of 'what might be'…

Above **BODMIN NORTH:** For many years the majority of the 'Southern' passenger services between Padstow, Wadebridge and Bodmin North were worked by a small fleet of ex-LSWR 'O2' tank engines shedded at Wadebridge. One of these, No 30236, waits to depart from the now-demolished Bodmin North station with its three-coach train on 18 May 1959. *Colour-Rail.com*

Below **WADEBRIDGE:** This general view of Wadebridge station in June 1966 is looking towards Padstow. Of particular note is the fine SR lattice-post signal. BR Class 03 diesel shunter No D2127 waits at the island platform with a special railway enthusiasts' brake-van charter. *Bernard Mills*

Above **WENFORDBRIDGE:** A general view of the sidings and 'Goods Depot' at Wenfordbridge. *Maurice Dart collection*

Below **WADEBRIDGE:** Steam returned to Wadebridge in September 2009! Having been unloaded onto a plinth of track very near to the shed at which it was based for more than 60 years, Beattie well tank No 30587 attracts admiring glances. The locomotive was brought by road from the BWR to Wadebridge as the centrepiece of a weekend of events and displays to commemorate the 175th anniversary of the original Bodmin & Wadebridge Railway. *Richard Jones*

Index to locations & locomotives

LOCATIONS

LOCOMOTIVES